MW00564036

Rem

Rem Koolhaas/OMA

KOOL

HAAS

Rem Koolhaas/OMA

teNeues

Editor in chief:
Paco Asensio

Editor and original texts:
Aurora Cuito

English translation:
William Bain

German translation:
Bettina Beck

French translation:
Michel Ficerai

Italian translation:
Giovanna Carnevali

Art direction:
Mireia Casanovas Soley

Graphic Design / Layout:
Emma Termes Parera and Soti Mas-Bagà

Published worldwide by teNeues Publishing Group
(except Spain, Portugal and South-America):

teNeues Book Division
Neuer Zollhof 1, 40221 Düsseldorf, Germany
Tel: 0049-(0)211-994597-0
Fax: 0049-(0)211-994597-40

teNeues Publishing Company
16 West 22ⁿᵈ Street, New York, N.Y., 10010, USA
Tel.: 001-212-627-9090
Fax: 001-212-627-9511

teNeues Publishing UK Ltd.
Aldwych House, 71/91 Aldwych
London WC2B 4HN, UK
Tel.: 0044-1892-837-171
Fax: 0044-1892-837-272

teNeues France S.A.R.L.
140, rue de la Croix Nivert
75015 Paris, France
Tel.: 0033-1-5576-6205
Fax: 0033-1-5576-6419

www.teneues.com

Editorial project:

© 2002 **LOFT** Publications
Domènech 7-9, 2° 2ª
08012 Barcelona, Spain
Tel.: 0034 932 183 099
Fax: 0034 932 370 060
e-mail: loft@loftpublications.com
www.loftpublications.com

Printed by:
Gráficas Anman. Sabadell, Spain.

September 2002

ISBN: 3-8238-5582-4

"Let us free architecture of the responsibilities that it can no longer assume and let us aggressively explore this newly released freedom." There is one primordial aim that moves the work of Rem Koolhaas, from the time of his writings to his projects and buildings, and this also determines the decisions on every scale, from the domestic to the urban, from the diagram to the detail: the discovery and empowerment of the relation that can be established between architecture and liberty. Koolhaas sets out to create new territories, physical and conceptual territories, of expansion, more than of regulation and control, experimental spaces where a wide variety of constructive logics can be applied. He defends chaos and the lack of moderation, and thus we see in his buildings walls that fold, ceilings that become floors, and combinations of materials that are highly imaginative and eclectic. Koolhaas's architecture is, definitely, a set of explicit contradictions and tensions.

The work of OMA, the studio headed by the Dutch architect and cofounded with Elia and Zoe Zenghelis and Mandelon Vriesendorp has generated some of the most interesting projects to appear on the scene in recent years. These projects range from fitting out universities like the Educatorium in Utrecht, where the students themselves propose and create the functional program, to shops like Prada in New York, where the clients make their purchases in the most interactive of spaces.

"Lasst uns die Architektur von der ihr unerträglich gewordenen Verantwortlichkeit befreien und uns diese neu erlangte Freiheit in aggressiver Art und Weise erforschen". Die Arbeit Rem Koolhaas', von seinen Schriften bis hin zu seinen Entwürfen und Gebäuden, besitzt die vorrangige Zielsetzung, die zwischen Architektur und Freiheit herstellbare Beziehung zu entdecken und zu verstärken. Dieses Ziel bestimmt die Entscheidungen auf allen Ebenen, vom Häuslichen bis zum Urbanen, vom Diagramm bis zum Detail. Koolhaas' Absicht ist die Schaffung neuer physischer und konzeptueller Territorien unter dem Aspekt der Ausdehnung statt der Regulierung und Kontrolle, die Schaffung experimenteller Räume, die vielfältige Anwendungsmöglichkeiten für konstruktive Vorstellungen bieten. Er verteidigt Chaos und Maßlosigkeit. Bei seinen Gebäuden biegen sich die Wände, Dächer werden zu Böden und die Kombination der Materialien ist phantasievoll und eklektizistisch. Seine Architektur ist letztendlich ein Bündel von Widersprüchen und ausdrücklich erwünschten Spannungen.

OMA, das Büro, das der niederländische Architekt leitet und das er zusammen mit Elia und Zoe Zenghelis und Mandelon Vriesendorp gründete, hat einige der interessantesten Projekte der letzten Jahre hervorgebracht. Diese reichen von universitären Einrichtungen wie dem Educatorium in Utrecht, wo die Studenten selbst das funktionelle Programm vorschlagen und formen, bis hin zu Geschäftsräumen wie Prada in New York, wo die Kunden in wahrhaftig interaktiven Räumen einkaufen können.

« Libérons l'architecture des responsabilités qu'elle ne peut plus assumer et explorons de façon agressive cette liberté encore naissante ». Un objectif primordial anime le travail de Rem Koolhaas, de ses écrits à ses projets ou ses constructions, et qui détermine les décisions, quel que soit le cadre, domestique ou urbain, du diagramme au détail : découvrir et promouvoir la relation qui peut s'établir entre l'architecture et la liberté. Koolhaas prétend créer de nouveaux territoires, physiques et conceptuels, d'expansion plus que de régulation et de contrôle. Des espaces expérimentaux susceptibles de se voir appliqué toute une diversité de logiques constructives. Il défend le chaos et la démesure. Ainsi, tous ses édifices affichent des murs pliables, des toits convertibles en sols et la combinaison de matériaux s'y révèle imaginative et éclectique. En définitive, son architecture est un foyer de contradictions et de tensions explicites.

L'œuvre d'OMA, l'étude dirigée par l'architecte hollandais et co-fondée avec Elia et Zoe Zenghelis et Mandelon Vriesendorp, a engendré quelques-uns des projets les plus intéressants de ces dernières années : depuis des installations universitaires comme l'Educatorium d'Utrecht, où les étudiants proposent et disposent eux-mêmes le programme fonctionnel, jusqu'à des boutiques, ainsi Prada à New York, dont les clients peuvent acheter dans des espaces effectivement interactifs.

"Liberiamo l'architettura dalle responsabilià che ormai non può più assumersi e abbiamo il coraggio di esplorare in modo aggressivo questa recente libertà acquisita". C'é un obiettivo primordiale che sta alla base di tutti i lavori di Rem Koolhaas, a partire dai sui scritti fino ad arrivare ai suoi progetti e edifici, e questo determina inoltre le decisioni che prende a tutte le scale, dal disegno degli interni sino al progetto urbano, dal diagramma al dettaglio: scoprire e potenziare la relazione che si può stabilire tra architettura e libertà. Koolhaas pretende di creare nuovi territori, fisici e concettuali, quelli in espansione, in cambiamento piuttosto che quelli di regolarizzazione e di controllo. Spazi sperimentali dove si possa applicare un' innumerevole variabile di logiche costruttive. Difende il caos e il "fuori-misura", allo stesso modo per cui nei suoi edifici si pareti si inclinano, le coperture si convertono in superfici calpestabili e la combinazione dei materiali é ricca di immaginazione ed eclettica. La sua architettura é, in definitiva, un raggruppamento di contraddizioni e tensioni esplicite.

L'opera di OMA, lo studio cappeggiato dall'architetto olandese e fondato insieme a Elia e Zoe Zenghelis e Mandelon Vriesendorp ha generato alcuni dei progetti più interessanti degli ultimi anni, dal polo universitario come ad esempio l'Educatorium di Utrecht in cui gli studenti propongono e conformano il programma funzionale, fino ad arrivare ai negozi come per esempio quello di Prada a New York in cui i clienti possono comprare in spazi realmente interattivi.

Villa Dall'Ava

Location: Saint Cloud, Paris, France
Date of construction: 1985-1991
Photography: Hisao Suzuki

The Villa Dall'Ava project, on the outskirts of Paris, constituted something of a challenge because it was difficult to integrate it into a suburban environment that was densely built up. The architects had to raise a house that would adapt itself to the neighboring constructions and simultaneously provide intimacy and offer views of the surrounding landscape. The builders opted for the creation of three strips that cross the site from east to west: the first was used as an asphalt accessway to the garage, the second is occupied by the residence, and the third was made into a gardened space with pedestrian access to the residence. The back part of the site was not built on, and the stands of trees there have been conserved. The domestic spaces are distributed on three levels. The garage and the rooms of the service personnel are on the ground floor. The kitchen and the living room are on the first floor. And the bedrooms occupy the bays on the top floor of the building. On the roof, from which Paris may be viewed, are two large terraces, one of which is gardened, the other having a swimming pool.

Das Projekt der Villa Dall'Ava in einem Vorort von Paris war aufgrund der Schwierigkeit, es in eine dicht besiedelte Gegend einzufügen, eine große Herausforderung. Die Architekten mussten ein an die Nachbargebäude angepasstes Haus bauen, das aber gleichzeitig Intimität bieten und Ausblick auf die umliegende Landschaft gewähren sollte. Sie entschieden sich für drei das Grundstück in ostwestlicher Richtung durchquerende Streifen. Der erste wurde als asphaltierter Eingang zur Garage benutzt, den zweiten nahm das Wohnhaus ein und der dritte wurde bepflanzt und beinhaltet einen Zugang für Fußgänger. Der hintere Teil des Grundstücks verblieb unbebaut und die vorhandenen Bäume wurden erhalten. Die Räume sind auf drei Ebenen verteilt: Die Garage und die Dienstzimmer wurden ins Erdgeschoss gelegt, Küche und Wohnzimmer ins erste Obergeschoss und die anderen Zimmer in den oberen Teil des Gebäudes. Auf dem Dach, von dem aus man einen großartigen Blick über Paris hat, befinden sich zwei Terrassen, eine davon bepflanzt, sowie ein Schwimmbad.

Le projet de la Villa Dall'Ava, dans la banlieue de Paris, constituait un réel défi de par sa difficile intégration dans un environnement suburbain densément construit. Les architectes devaient construire une maison susceptible de se marier aux constructions voisines tout en offrant intimité et vues sur le paysage environnant. L'option fut prise de créer trois franges entrecroisant le terrain d'est en ouest : la première fut utilisée pour offrir un accès asphalté au garage, la seconde était réservée à la demeure et la troisième fut aménagée en jardin proposant un accès piétonnier à la maison. La partie arrière du terrain fut laissée en l'état, conservant les arbres d'origine. Les espaces domestiques se distribuent selon trois niveaux : le garage et les pièces de services occupent le rez-de-chaussée, la cuisine et les salles de séjour le premier étage et les chambres occupent deux volumes de la partie supérieure de la construction. Sur le toit, qui permet de profiter d'un panorama magnifique sur Paris, ont été disposées deux terrasses, dont une aménagée en jardin, et une piscine.

Il progetto della Villa Dall'Ava, nella periferia di Parigi, consisteva in una sfida a causa della sua difficile integrazione con l'intorno urbano densamente costruito. Gli architetti dovevano sollevare una casa per adattarsi a quelle vicine e allo stesso tempo per trovare un giusto equilibrio tra intimità ed esterno, che offre un fantastico panorama sul paesaggio circostante. Si optò per creare tre stecche che incrociassero l'area di progetto, secondo l'orientazione est-ovest: la prima é destinata all'accesso asfaltato e al garage, la seconda alla residenza mentre la terza all'accesso pedonale alla casa. La parte retrostante del terreno non venne costruita e vennero conservati gli alberi esistenti. Gli spazi domestici si distribuiscono su tre livelli. Il garage e i servizi sono ubicati al piano terra, la cucina e il soggiorno al primo piano mentre le stanze da letto occupano due volumi che fuoriescono dal volume totale. Sulla pianta coperture, dalla quale si può ammirare una fantastica vista di Parigi, vennero collocate due terrazze, di cui una con giardino me tre l'altra con piscina.

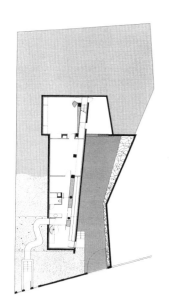

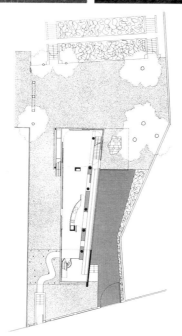

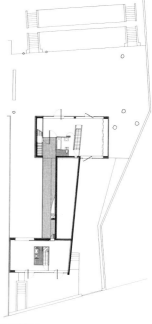

Ground floor
Erdgeschoss
Rez-de-chaussée
Piano terra

First floor
Erstes Obergeschoss
Premier étage
Piano primo

Second floor
Zweites Obergeschoss
Deuxième étage
Piano secondo

0 1 2

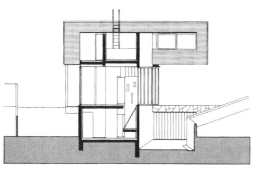
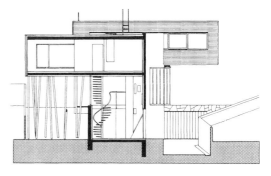

Cross sections
Querschnitte
Sections transversale
Sezioni trasversale

0   1   2

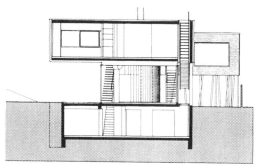

Cross section
Querschnitt
Sections transversale
Sezione trasversale

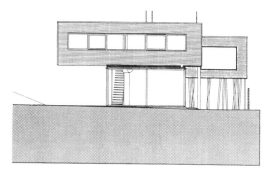

Elevation
Aufriss
Élévation
Prospetto

Kunsthal

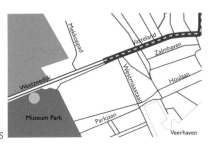

Location: Museum Park, Westzeedijk 341, Rotterdam, The Netherlands
Date of construction: 1992
Photography: Christian Richters

Located between an extremely busy avenue and the zone limiting the south side of Museum Park, the Kunsthal is obliged to confront a double situation: one of the façades looks onto the park, a context of peace and quiet; but the other, sited on a higher level, bears the brunt of the bustle on a major city artery. The building strikes us as a continuous circuit that ceaselessly crosses the different exhibition rooms through the use of ramps, corridors, and stairs. A pedestrian ramp divides the whole in a longitudinal direction, joining street and park. The exterior section, which admits the public, then becomes the integrating part of the interior route of the art gallery. Parallel to this passageway, another ramp has been placed, going down, and at the intersection of these two pieces is the main entrance to the place. When museum-goers have finished their visit, they are provided with access to an outdoor gardened terrace that offers magnificent views of the surroundings. The building combines the use of a wide variety of materials, such as metal, translucent glass, wood, or stone. This eclecticism is also present in the structure, which does not follow a modular arrangement.

Zwischen einer stark befahrenen Verkehrsader und dem Museum Park liegend, an den sie im Süden angrenzt, liegt die Kunsthal zwischen zwei Extremen: Eine der Fassaden liegt, ruhig und beschaulich, zum Park hin, während die andere, weiter oben gelegene Bereich, auf eine laute Straße hinaus geht. Das Gebäude stellt eine Kreislinie dar, auf der die verschiedenen Ausstellungsräume durch Rampen, Flure und Treppen durchkreuzt sind. Eine Fußgängerrampe teilt den Komplex in Längsrichtung und verbindet die Straße mit dem Park. Der äußere, der Öffentlichkeit zugängliche Abschnitt wird zum Bestandteil der innen gelegenen Ausstellungsräume. Parallel zu diesem Durchgang verläuft eine weitere, abwärts führende Rampe und am Schnittpunkt der beiden befindet sich der Haupteingang zum ersten Raum. Hat der Besucher seinen Rundgang beendet, kann er auf eine bepflanzte Dachterrasse hinaustreten, von der aus man einen großartigen Ausblick auf die Umgebung hat. Das Gebäude vereint in sich vielfältige Materialien wie Metall, Holz oder Stein. Dieser Eklektizismus wird auch an der Struktur deutlich, die keiner modularen Ordnung folgt.

Situé entre une avenue au trafic intense et la zone jouxtant au sud avec le Museum Park, le Kunsthal est confronté à une situation duale : une des façades est orientée vers le parc, un espace de tranquillité et de contemplation, l'autre, en revanche, située à un niveau supérieur, s'affronte avec un point de passage bruyant. L'édifice se présente comme un circuit continu qui traverse les différentes salles d'exposition à l'aide de rampes, de couloirs et d'escaliers. Une rampe piétonnière divise l'ensemble dans le sens longitudinal, connectant la voie et le parc. Le tronçon extérieur, ouvert au public, devient une partie intégrante du parcours intérieur de la galerie d'art. Parallèle à ce parcours, une autre rampe d'inclinaison inverse traverse l'espace et, à leur intersection, se trouve l'entrée principale de la première salle. Lorsque l'usager termine la visite, il peut accéder à une terrasse paysagère extérieure, sur le toit, depuis laquelle s'offrent à lui de magnifiques vues sur les alentours. Le bâtiment combine une grande variété de matériaux tels le métal, le verre translucide, le bois ou la pierre. Cet éclectisme se manifeste tout autant dans la structure, qui ne suit aucun ordonnancement modulaire.

Ubicato in una strada di intenso traffico e la zona che limita la parte sud con il Museum Park, il Kunsthal si trova di fronte a una doppia situazione: una delle facciate è orientata verso il parco, area tranquilla e dedita alla contemplazione, mentre l'altra, ubicata a livello superiore ha difronte un passaggio molto trafficato. L'edificio si presenta come un circuito continuo che incrocia di volta in volta le differenti sale espositive mediante rampe, corridoi e scale. Una rampa pedonale divide il complesso in senso longitudinale, cha si allaccia alla passeggiata con il parco. La parte esterna, aperta al pubblico, si converte in una parte integrante del percorso interno della galleria d'arte. Parallela a questo passaggio, scende un'altra rampa con un'inclinazione opposta a quella precedente, e la intersezione di queste avviene nell'entrata principale della prima sala. Quando il visitatore termina la propria visita può accedere alla terrazza esterna con giardino nella copertura dalla quale si può godere di una bellissima vista dell'intorno. L'edificio è una miscellanea di materiali, come il metallo, il cristallo translucido, il legno e la pietra. Questo eclecticismo si manifesta inoltre nella struttura, che non segue un'ordine modulare.

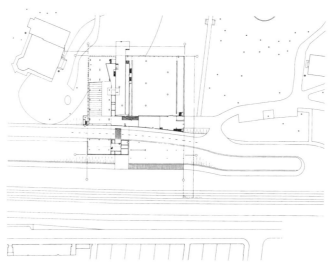

Plan Grundriss
Niveau Pianta

0 6 12

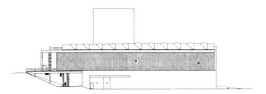
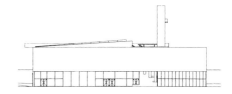

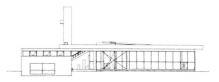

Elevations
Aufrisse
Élévations
Prospetti

0   3   6

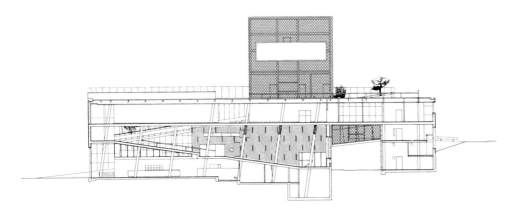

Longitudinal section
Längsschnitt
Section longitudinale
Sezione longitudinale

0   2   4

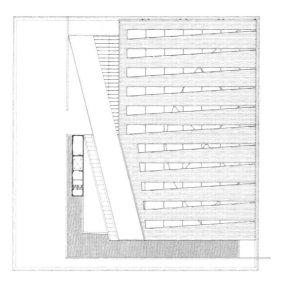

Roof
Dach
Toit
Copertura

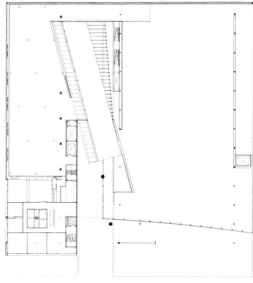

Second floor
Zweites Obergeschoss
Deuxième étage
Piano secondo

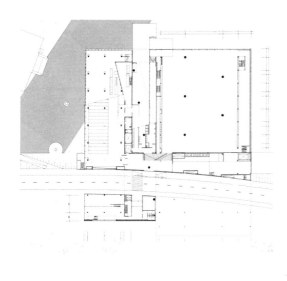

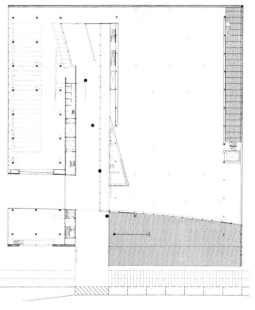

Plan   Grundriss
Niveau   Pianta

  0 5 10

First floor   Premier étage
Erstes Obergeschoss   Piano primo

0 4 8

Congrexpo

Location: Euralille, Lille, France
Date of construction: 1990-1994
Photography: Christian Richters

The project by Rem Koolhaas described here involves an urban restructuring. It was done in the French town of Lille in collaboration with other architects of some international renown, people such as Jean Nouvel, Gilles Clément, and Christian de Portzamparc. The project, which is in fact located inside the old city walls between the historical city center and the outskirts, is a species of hybrid building 984 feet long. It has a clear, three-bay distribution: there is a room for rock concerts (Zenith), with a capacity for 6000 spectators; a congressional center (Congres), with three auditoriums, exhibition rooms, a banquet area, and kitchens; and a large exhibit space (Expo) of a surface area of 215,278 square feet, which subdivides into three equal areas. The complex also includes a large covered garage. The different building programs, integrated under a single roof, are interconnecting and, in some cases, include the option of merging and carrying out new functions. The unit having one roof is emphasized by the use of materials in similar tones of gray, materials like cement, steel, and a medium gauge metallic screen.

Der Beitrag von Rem Koolhaas steht im Zusammenhang mit der Umstrukturierung der französischen Stadt Lille, an der weitere international anerkannte Architekten wie Jean Nouvel, Gilles Clément oder Christian de Portzamparc mitwirkten. Das innerhalb der alten Stadtmauer zwischen dem alten Stadtkern und der Peripherie befindliche Projekt besteht aus einem hybriden Gebäude von 300 m Länge und einer klaren Aufteilung in drei Elemente. Es setzt sich zusammen aus einem Saal für Rockkonzerte (Zenith) mit Platz für 6000 Zuschauer, einem aus drei Auditorien, Ausstellungsräumen und einem Bankett- und Küchenbereich bestehenden Kongresszentrum (Congres), und schließlich einem Ausstellungspalast (Expo) mit einer Fläche von 20.000 m², die in drei gleich große Bereiche unterteilt werden kann. Außerdem beinhaltet der Komplex ein Parkhaus. Die verschiedenen Programme des unter einem einzigen Dach untergebrachten Baus sind miteinander verbunden. In einigen Fällen können sogar zwei oder mehr Räume zu einem neuen Zweck miteinander verbunden werden. Diese Einheit verschiedener Gebäude unter demselben Dach wird durch die Verwendung von Materialien von ähnlicher Graufärbung wie Beton, Stahl und Metallnetz betont.

La participation de Rem Koolhaas s'inscrit dans le cadre de la restructuration urbanistique entreprise dans la ville de Lille, à laquelle purent collaborer d'autres architectes au prestige international tels Jean Nouvel, Gilles Clément ou Christian de Portzamparc. Le projet, situé à l'intérieur du périmètre des anciens murs de la ville, entre le centre historique et la périphérie, est une construction hybride de 300 mètres de long et présente une distribution claire en trois éléments : une salle de concerts de rock (Zenith), d'une capacité de 6 000 spectateurs, un palais des congrès (Congres), composé de trois auditoriums, de salles d'exposition, d'une zone pour les banquets et de cuisines, et enfin d'un palais des expositions (Expo), d'une superficie de 20 000 m² subdivisibles en trois zones similaires. Le complexe inclut aussi un vaste parking couvert. Les différents programmes du projet, intégralement situés sous une couverte unique, s'interconnectent et, dans certains cas, deux ou plusieurs espaces peuvent même s'unir pour répondre à de nouveaux besoins. L'unité apportée par le toit unique se voit soulignée par l'emploi de matériaux aux tonalités grisâtres semblables, ainsi le béton, l'acier et la maille métallique.

Il lavoro di Rem Koolhaas di riconosce nella riforma a livello urbanistico che si portò a termine nella città francese di Lille, in cui collaborarono altri architetti di fama internazionale come Jean Nouvel, Gilles Clément o Christian de Portzamparc. Il progetto, che è ubicato dentro il perimetro delle antiche mure della città, tra il centro storico e le periferia, è un edificio ibrido di 300 metri di longitudine e ha una distribuzione chiara di tre elementi: una sala per concerti rock (Zenith), con una capacità di 6000 spettatori, un centro congressi (Congres), composto da tre auditori, sale espositive, una zona per banchetti e ricevimenti con cucine; e inoltre un palazzo di esposizioni (Expo), con una superficie di 20 mila m², suddivisibile in tre aree uguali. Il complesso include inoltre un grande parcheggio al coperto. I diversi programmi del complesso, ubicati integral-mente sotto un'unica copertura, si connettono reciprocamente e in alcuni casi si possono unire due di questi o più per ospitare nuove funzioni. L'unità che apporta un'unica copertura viene enfatizzata dalla utilizzazione di materiali con tonalità di grigio simili tra loro, come il cemento, l'acciaio e la maglia metallica.

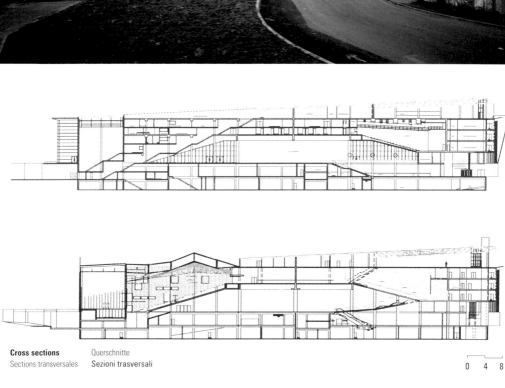

Cross sections   Querschnitte
Sections transversales   **Sezioni trasversali**

0   4   8

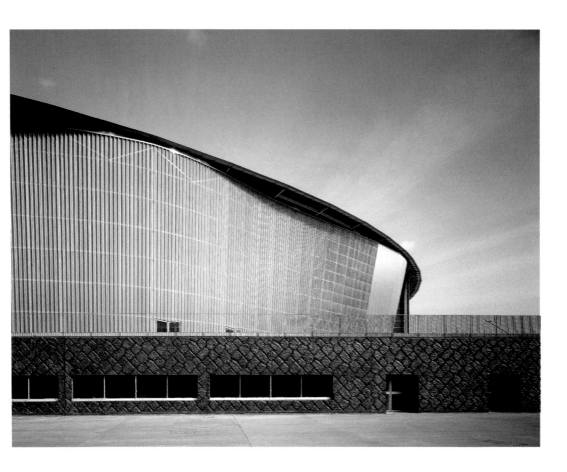

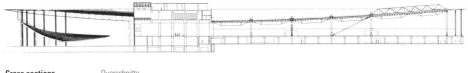

Cross sections   Querschnitte
Sections transversales   Sezioni trasversali

0   4   8

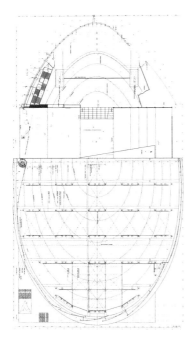

Roof   Dach
Toit   **Copertura**

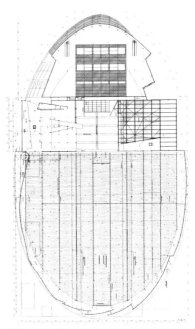

Ceiling   Decke
Plafond   **Soffitto**

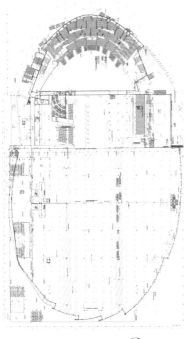

Ground floor   Erdgeschoss
Rez-de-chaussée   **Piano terra**

0   5   10

House in the Forest

Location: The Netherlands
Date of construction: 1992-1994
Photography: Christian Richters

The 53,820-square-foot lot on which this building is sited is part of a large pine woods on a moraine that dates back to the end of the Ice Age. The unstable conditions of the foundation and current local urban codes that keep buildings at least 13 feet from the access road were determining factors in the project's development. The domestic program was also a conditioning aspect of the final design: two well-delineated zones were called for, one for the couple who permanently live in the house and another for their three children, who come to visit their parents from time to time. In order to maintain a kind of lived-in look during the absences of the younger generation, two independent spaces were built, one on top of the other. These, in turn, are made mutually available through a large ramp that serves as an interface element. The children's area includes a bay behind a surrounding wall that defines a series of rooms en suite with patios. The floating ceiling supports the transparent volume of the parents' space. This establishes a relation with the exterior that varies according to the function and orientation of each of the spaces.

La parcelle de cinq mille mètres carrés accueillant cette demeure appartient à une vaste pinède reposant sur une moraine remontant à la fin de l'ère glaciaire. Les conditions de fondations instables et les normes urbanistiques locales, interdisant de dépasser une hauteur de quatre mètres au-delà du niveau de la route d'accès, ont été déterminantes dans le développement du projet. Le programme intérieur a également conditionné la conception finale : deux zones différenciées étaient nécessaires, une pour le couple résidant de façon permanente dans la maison et l'autre pour leurs trois filles, visiteuses occasionnelles de leurs parents. Dans l'intention de dissimuler la certitude de ces absences, deux pièces indépendantes ont été créées, disposées l'une sur l'autre, qui pour autant jouissent de moments d'interaction en étant reliées par une rampe. La partie occupée par les filles dispose d'un mur d'enceinte qui définit une série de pièces et de patios. Sa couverte flottante soutient le volume transparent des parents qui établit une relation avec l'extérieur, évoluant selon la fonction et l'orientation de chacun des espaces.

Das fünftausend Quadratmeter große Grundstück, auf dem sich das Wohnhaus befindet, ist Teil eines großen Pinienwalds, der auf einer eiszeitlichen Endmöräne liegt. Die Instabilität der Fundamente und die örtlichen städtebaulichen Vorschriften, die eine Bauhöhe von mehr als vier Metern über der Höhe der Zugangsstraße unmöglich machten, gehörten zu den Prämissen der Projektentwicklung. Doch auch die Anforderungen, die an das Innere des Hauses gestellt wurden, bestimmten die endgültige Gestaltung. Es wurden zwei unterschiedliche Bereiche benötigt, einer für das Paar, das das Haus ständig bewohnt, und ein weiterer für die drei Töchter, die ihre Eltern nur gelegentlich besuchen. Damit das Gebäude auch während der Abwesenheit der Kinder einen bewohnten Eindruck macht, wurden zwei selbstständige, übereinanderliegende Teile geschaffen, die durch verschiedene Elemente wie beispielsweise eine Rampe miteinander verbunden sind. Der von den Töchtern bewohnte Trakt besteht aus einer Reihe von Zimmern und Höfen, die von einer Mauer eingefasst sind. Auf dem schwebenden Dach liegt der transparente Bereich der Eltern, der seinerseits eine je nach Funktion und Ausrichtung der verschiedenen Räume variierende Beziehung mit dem Äußeren eingeht.

La parcella di cinquemila metri quadrati dove si ubicò questa casa appartiene a un grande bosco di pini che si adagiano un una area che viene datata circa verso la fine dell'Era Glaciale. Le instabili condizioni di cementazione e le leggi urbanistiche locali che non permettevano di oltrepassare i quattro metri in altezza dalla quota stradale di accesso, furono le regole che determinarono lo sviluppo del progetto. Inoltre anche il programma dello sviluppo degli interni condizionò il disegno finale: si richiedevano zone distinte, una per la coppia che risiede permanentemente in casa e l'altra per le tre figlie che vanno a trovare i genitori occasionalmente. Con l'intenzione di dissimulare la certezza delle loro assenze, si crearono due parti indipendenti, collocate una sull'altra, che a loro volta possono godere dei momenti di interazione e sono relazionate da una grande rampa. Il corpo dell'edificio occupato dalle figlie consiste in un muro perimetrale che definisce una serie di soggiorni e di patii. Il tetto sospeso sostiene il volume trasparente dei genitori che a sua volta stabilisce una relazione con l'esterno che varia in funzione dell'orientamento di ciscuno degli spazi.

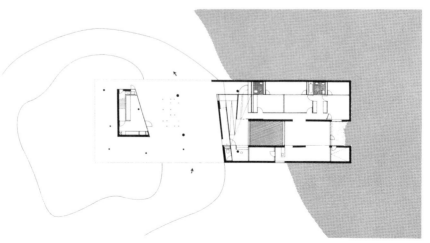

Ground floor   Erdgeschoss
Rez-de-chaussée   Piano terra

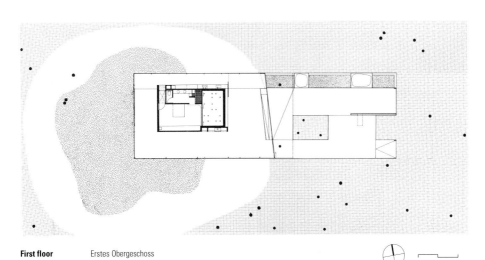

First floor   Erstes Obergeschoss
Premier étage   Piano primo

0   3   6

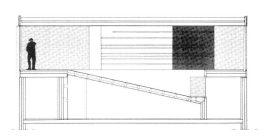

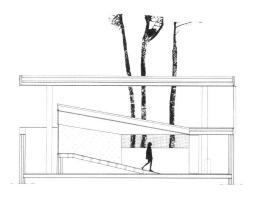

Cross sections
Querschnitte
Sections transversales
Sezioni trasversali

0 1 2

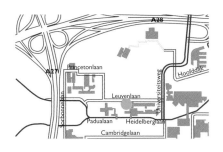

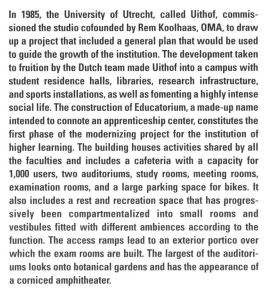

Educatorium

Location: Leuvenlaan 19, Utrecht, The Netherlands
Date of construction: 1992-1997
Photography: Christian Richters

In 1985, the University of Utrecht, called Uithof, commissioned the studio cofounded by Rem Koolhaas, OMA, to draw up a project that included a general plan that would be used to guide the growth of the institution. The development taken to fruition by the Dutch team made Uithof into a campus with student residence halls, libraries, research infrastructure, and sports installations, as well as fomenting a highly intense social life. The construction of Educatorium, a made-up name intended to connote an apprenticeship center, constitutes the first phase of the modernizing project for the institution of higher learning. The building houses activities shared by all the faculties and includes a cafeteria with a capacity for 1,000 users, two auditoriums, study rooms, meeting rooms, examination rooms, and a large parking space for bikes. It also includes a rest and recreation space that has progressively been compartmentalized into small rooms and vestibules fitted with different ambiences according to the function. The access ramps lead to an exterior portico over which the exam rooms are built. The largest of the auditoriums looks onto botanical gardens and has the appearance of a corniced amphitheater.

1985 beauftragte die Uithof genannte Universität von Utrecht das Büro von Rem Koolhaas, OMA, mit dem Entwurf für einen Generalplan, der die Entwicklung dieser wachsenden Institution steuern sollte. Das holländische Team hat Uithof zu einem Campus mit Studentenwohnheimen, Bibliotheken, Forschungs- und Sporteinrichtungen gemacht und darüber hinaus den Komplex mit intensivem sozialem Leben erfüllt. Der Bau des Educatoriums – der Name wurde erfunden, um eine „Lernfabrik" zu beschreiben – ist die erste Phase des Modernisierungsprojekts der Universität. Das Gebäude beherbergt von allen Fakultäten gemeinsam benutzte Einrichtungen: Eine Cafeteria für tausend Gäste, zwei Auditorien, Studien-, Tagungs- und Prüfungsräume sowie einen großen Fahrradparkplatz. Außerdem wurde ein in kleine Säle und Vestibüle unterteilter Ruhebereich integriert, dessen Raum von den Benutzern je nach Zweck gestaltet werden kann. Die Zugangsrampen führen zu einem äußeren Säulengang, über dem sich die Examensräume befinden. Das größere der Auditorien erscheint wie ein überkragendes Amphitheater und bietet Ausblicke auf die botanischen Gärten.

En 1985, l'Université d'Utrecht, baptisée Uithof, commanda au cabinet de Rem Koolhaas, OMA, l'étude du projet d'un plan général afin de guider la croissance de l'institution. Le développement réalisé par l'équipe hollandaise a converti la Uithof en un campus comprenant des résidences étudiantes, des bibliothèques, des infrastructures pour la recherche, des installations sportives èt a, par surcroît, conféré à l'ensemble une intense vie sociale. La construction de l'Educatorium, un nom inventé qui tend à qualifier une « usine » à apprentissage, constitue la première phase du projet de modernisation de l'université. L'édifice héberge des fonctions communes à toutes les facultés et accueille une cafétéria d'une capacité de mille usagers, deux auditoriums, des salles d'études et d'examen et un vaste parc de stationnement pour bicyclettes. L'ensemble comprend également une aire de repos qui a été compartimentée en petites salles et vestibules, auxquels les usagers confèrent une atmosphère différente selon la fonction attendue. Les rampes d'accès mènent à un portique extérieur au-dessus duquel ont été placées les salles d'examen. Le principal auditorium dispose de vues sur les jardins botaniques et s'apparente à un amphithéâtre projeté.

Nel 1985 la università di Utrecht, chiamata Uithof, incaricò allo studio di Rem Koolhaas, OMA, la progettazione di un piano regolatore che dovesse guidare la crescita dell'istituto. Lo sviluppo di questo compito portato a termine dallo studio olandese ha convertito Uithof in un campus con residenze per studenti, biblioteche, infrastrutture per la riceca e sviluppo, attrezzature sportive e inoltre ha dotato il complesso di un'intensa vita sociale. La costruzione dell'Educatorium, un nome inventato che ha l'ambizione di qualificare un'industria dell'apprendimento, costituisce la prima fase del progetto di modernizzazione dell'università. L'edificio alberga funzioni condivise tra tutte le facoltà e accoglie una caffetteria con una capienza per mille persone; due auditori, sale di studio e di riunione, aule per esami e un grande parcheggio per biciclette. Si incluse inoltre un'area di riposo che si è divisa successivamente in piccole aule e sale di ingresso a seconda dei diversi utenti e dalle loro diverse necessità di funzioni richieste. Le rampe di accesso conducono a un porticato esterno in cima al quale sono ubicate le sale dedicate agli esami. L'auditorio più grande possiede viste a tutti i giardini botanici e sembra un anfiteatro a sbalzo.

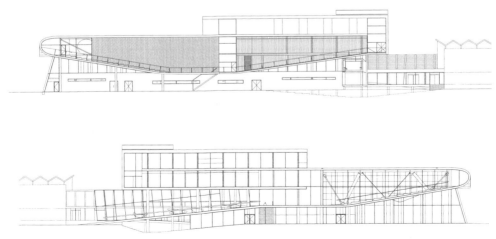

Elevations   Aufrisse
Élévations   Prospetti

0   4   8

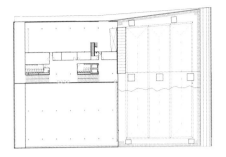

Third floor
Drittes Obergeschoss
Troisième étage
Piano terzo

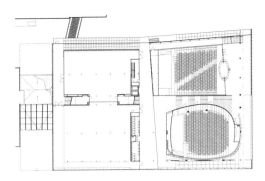

Second floor
Zweites Obergeschoss
Deuxième étage
Piano secondo

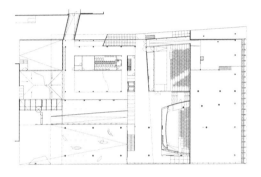

First floor
Erstes Obergeschoss
Premier étage
Piano primo

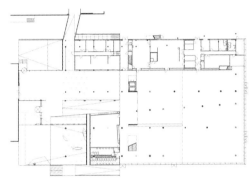

Ground floor
Erdgeschoss
Rez-de-chaussée
Piano terra

0   3   6

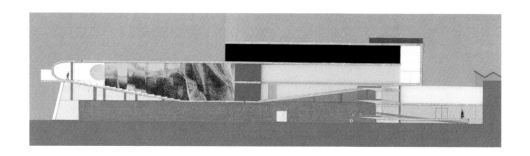

Elevations   Aufrisse
Élévations   **Prospetti**

Prada Shop

Location: 575 Broadway, New York, USA
Date of construction: 2002
Photography: Michael Moran

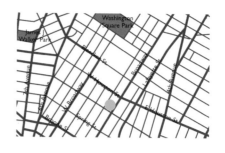

Any fashion firm that has a proper amount of amour propre must update its selling points quite as often as the apparel it markets. Besides, stores act as a comercial inducement and there are progressively more companies in the sector that commission their designs to internationally prestigious architects. The Italian brand Prada has put its money on Rem Koolhaas, who in turn has counted on the collaboration of the ARO Studio, to build its new New York Soho boutique. And this, as it happens, is a luxurious place for an innovative and interactive project that includes the latest technologies and can constantly transform itself. The building has two floors and a basement destined for use as a storage area. The ironwork that separates the ground floor from the first floor is evocative of a tectonic plate: it molds itself into a large staircase around which clients may sit down and try on shoes, in the process molding the floor of the next level up. AMO, OMA's parallel studio, was commissioned to create the computerized accessories. An example of what they came up with in this sphere are the computers that make it possible to vary the opacity of the dressing rooms or to project videos onto some of the walls.

Jedes angesehene Modehaus muss seine Verkaufsräume genauso häufig aktualisieren wie die Kleidungsstücke, die es verkauft. Außerdem fungieren die Geschäfte als kommerzieller Anziehungspunkt, sodass immer mehr Unternehmen in dieser Branche international anerkannte Architekten mit dem Design ihrer Geschäftsräume beauftragen. Die italienische Marke Prada setzte bei ihrer neuen Boutique im New Yorker Stadtteil Soho auf Rem Koolhaas und die Mitwirkung des Büros ARO. In dieser Luxuslage entstand ein innovatives und interaktives Projekt, das die jüngsten Technologien umfasst und zu konstanter Transformation fähig ist. Das Gebäude besteht aus zwei Stockwerken und einem Untergeschoss, das als Lager benutzt wird. Die Treppe zwischen dem Erdgeschoss und dem ersten Obergeschoss erinnert an eine tektonische Platte und bietet in ihrer Biegung Raum für Kunden, die Schuhe anprobieren möchten. Anschließend führt die Treppe wie eine gigantische Welle weiter nach oben und bildet den Fußboden der darüber liegenden Ebene. AMO, das Partnerbüro von OMA, übernahm die computergesteuerte Ausstattung. So kann beispielsweise die Durchsichtigkeit der Umkleidekabinen verändert oder es können in einigen Abteilungen Videos vorgeführt werden.

Toute entreprise de mode qui se respecte doit mettre ses points de vente au goût du jour aussi souvent que les vêtements qu'elle vend. De plus, les boutiques remplissent un rôle publicitaire et de plus en plus de ces sociétés confient la conception de leurs locaux à des architectes de prestige international. La griffe italienne Prada a misé sur Rem Koolhaas, qui a pu compter avec la contribution de l'étude AMO, dans sa nouvelle boutique du Soho new-yorkais. Un emplacement de luxe pour un projet novateur et interactif, incorporant les ultimes technologies et capable de se métamorphoser constamment. L'édifice comporte deux niveaux et un sous-sol, destiné au stock. La structure forgée séparant le rez-de-chaussée évoque une plaque tectonique dont les contours donnent naissance à un vaste escalier, où les clients peuvent s'asseoir et essayer les chaussures, pour monter à nouveau comme une gigantesque vague et former le sol du niveau supérieur. AMO, l'étude parallèle à OMA, fut chargé de créer les accessoires informatiques, notamment ceux permettant de faire varier l'opacité des cabines d'essayage ou de projeter des vidéos sur certaines partitions.

Qualunque firma della moda che tiene ambizione debe attualizzare i suoi punti vendita tanto frequentemente come le presentazioni stagionali di capi che presenta. Inoltre, i negozi rivestono il ruolo ri richiamo commerciale e sempre più frequentemente le imprese di settore incaricano il disegno dei propri locali ad architetti di prestigio e fama internazionale. La marca italiana Prada ha scommesso su Rem Koolhaas, che ha collaborato con lo studio ARO, per la sua nuova boutique del Soho newyorkino. Una posizione di lusso per un progetto nuovo e interattivo, che incorpora le ultime tecnologie ed è in grado di trasformarsi costantemente. L'edificio è su due piani e un semi interrato destinato a magazzino. Il pavimento che separa la pianta piano terra dal primo piano richiama una placca tettonica e gira su se stesso per dare origine a una grande scalinata, dove i clienti si possono sedere e provare le scarpe, per poi scendere successivamente come un'onda gigantesca e aper quindi diventare pavimento del piano superiore. AMO, lo studio parallelo a OMA; su incaricato di creare gli accessori informatici, come per esempio quelli che permettono di variare l'opacità dei camerini o di proiettare video in alcune pareti divisorie.

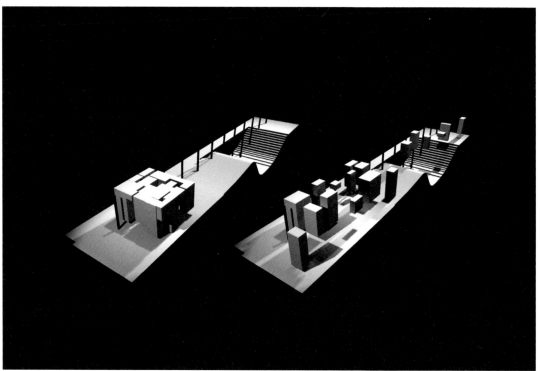

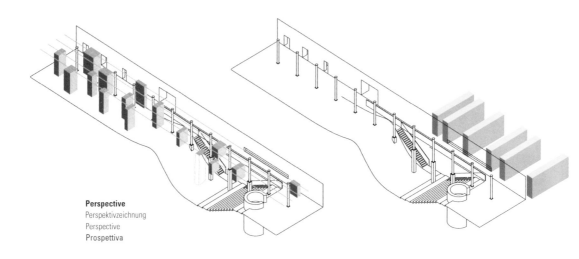

Perspective
Perspektivzeichnung
Perspective
Prospettiva

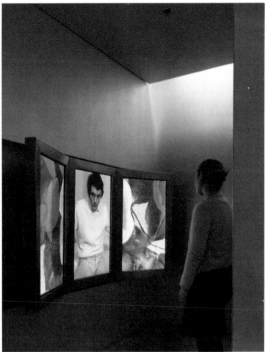

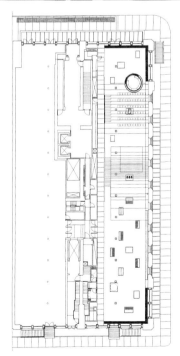

Ground floor
Erdgeschoss
Rez-de-chaussée
Piano terra

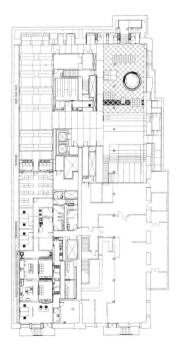

First floor
Erstes Obergeschoss
Premier étage
Piano primo

0 4 8

Guggenheim Museums

Location: 3355 Las Vegas Boulevard South, Las Vegas, USA
Date of construction: 2002
Photography: Michael Moran

The Las Vegas Guggenheim and the Guggenheim-Hermitage Museum are two museums that the foundation has opened in the city of the casinos, in installations that belong to the surprising Venetian Hotel. The Venetian recreates the Italian city to the point of bringing you the canals and gondolas to take you to some of the rooms. Guggenheim Las Vegas has been conceived to present contemporary art exhibits: painting, sculpture, architecture, design, and multimedia art. In the main room, accessed by a spectacular revolving door 68.89 feet high, an escalator was installed to accompany the large lime green staircase that descends to the lower level. A large skylight introduces natural light that is filtered by a large mural that reproduces the emblematic Sixtine Chapel scene by Michelangelo. The Guggenheim-Hermitage Museum came out of the collaboration of the two institutions as a new way to program modern art exhibits. The building, located in front of the hotel, is constructed of metal permanently covered in a layer of rust, which brings to mind the velvet curtains of the museum in Saint Petersburg and which also contrasts beautifully with the smooth birch wood floors.

Das Guggenheim Las Vegas und das Museum Guggenheim-Hermitage sind die beiden von der Stiftung in der Kasinohochburg eröffneten Museen, die zum Komplex des spektakulären Hotels The Venetian gehören. Es empfindet die italienische Stadt so getreu nach, dass als Verbindung zwischen einigen der Zimmer sogar Kanäle und Gondeln fungieren. Das Guggenheim Las Vegas wurde für die Präsentation von Ausstellungen zeitgenössischer Kunst konzipiert: Malerei, Bildhauerei, Architektur, Design und Multimedia-Kunst. Im Hauptsaal, in den man durch eine spektakuläre 21 m hohe Drehtür gelangt, wurden die in die untere Ebene führenden Rolltreppen und eine große limonengrüne Freitreppe untergebracht. Ein großer Lichthof lässt natürliches Licht einströmen, das von einem großen Wandgemälde gefiltert wird, das Michelangelos Deckenfresko der Sixtinischen Kapelle reproduziert. Das Museum Guggenheim Hermitage entstand aus der Zusammenarbeit der beiden Einrichtungen zur Planung von Ausstellungen zeitgenössischer Kunst. Das dem Hotel gegenüberliegende Gebäude ist aus Corten-Stahl gebaut. Dieses Metall ist permanent von einer Rostschicht überzogen, die an die Samtvorhänge des St. Petersburger Museums erinnert und außerdem einen reizvollen Kontrast zu den glatten Böden und Dächern aus Ahornholz bildet.

Le Guggenheim Las Vegas et le Musée Guggenheim-Hermitage sont les deux musées que la fondation a ouverts dans la ville des casinos, dans les installations du surprenant hôtel The Venetian qui recrée la ville italienne au point de compter canaux et gondoles pour relier certaines chambres. Le Guggenheim Las Vegas a été conçu afin de présenter des expositions d'art contemporain : peinture, sculpture, architecture, design et art multimédia. Dans la salle principale, accessible par une spectaculaire porte pivotante de 21 mètres de haut, ont été disposés des escaliers mécaniques et un grand escalier de couleur vert lime, qui descendent vers les niveaux inférieurs. Une ample claire-voie introduit la lumière naturelle qui demeure filtrée par un grand mural reproduisant la scène emblématique de la Chapelle Sixtine de Michel-Ange. Le musée Guggenheim-Hermitage a surgi de la coopération des deux institutions pour programmer des expositions d'art moderne. Le bâtiment, situé face à l'hôtel, est construit en acier corten, un métal recouvert de façon permanente d'une couche d'oxyde qui évoque les tentures de velours rouge du musée de Saint Petersbourg et offre un contraste avec les sols et les plafonds lisses, en bois d'érable

Il Guggenheim Las Vegas e il Museo Guggenheim-Hermitage sono i due musei che la Fondazione ha aperto nella città dei casinò, presso le installazioni del sorpendente Hotel The Venetian che raffigura la città italiana fino al punto di utilizzare i canali e le gondole per metter in comunicazione alcune stanze. Il Guggenheim Las Vegas venne concepito per presentare esposizioni di arte contemporanea: pittura, scultura, architettura, design e multimedia. Nella sala principale, alla quale si accede tramite una spettacolare porta pivotante di 21 metri di altezza, vennero collocare le scale mobili e una grande scalinata di color verde lima che scende al livello inferiore. Un gran lucernario lascia penetrare luce naturale che viene filtrata da un grande murales che riproduce l'emblematica scena della Cappella Sistina di Michelangelo. Il museo Guggenheim-Hermitage nacque dalla collaborazione delle due istituzioni al fine di programmare e organizzare esposizioni di arte moderna. L'edificio, ubicato di fronte all'hotel, è costruito in acciaio corten, metallo ricoperto costantemente da uno strato di ossido che richiama le tende vellutate del museo di San Pietroburgo e che contrasta con i pavimenti e i tetti lisci , in legno d'acero.

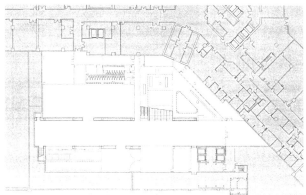

Ground floor   Erdgeschoss
Rez-de-chaussée   Piano terra

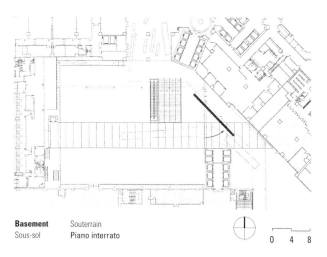

Basement   Souterrain
Sous-sol   Piano interrato

0   4   8

Chronology of works 1989-2002

1989 Sea Terminal, Zeebrugge, Belgium. Competition.
Museum Park, Rotterdam, The Netherlands.
Nexus World Housing Fukuoka, Japan.
OMA: The First Decade, Rotterdam, The Netherlands.
ZKM (Center for Art and Media Technology), Karlsruhe, Germany.
Project for an Office City, Frankfurt, Germany. Competition.
Très Grande Bibliothèque, Paris, France. Competition.
Sports Complex, Groningen, The Netherlands.
Staad aan de Stroom, Antwerp, Belgium. Competition.
Video Bus Stop, Groningen, The Netherlands.

1990 OMA: Fin de siècle, Paris, France. Exhibition.
Rem Koolhaas, OMA in Lille, Lille, France. Exhibition.
Energieen, Amsterdam, The Netherlands. Exhibition.
Palm Bay Seafront Hotel and Convention, Agadir, Morocco. Competition.
Hilton Hotel, The Hague, The Netherlands. Project.
Souterrain, The Hague, The Netherlands.
Congrexpo, Lille, France.
OMA: Recent Projects, Barcelona, Spain. Exhibition.

1991 Mission Grand Axe, La Défense, Paris, France. Competition.
Duisburg Urban Planning, Duisburg, Germany. Competition.
Transferia, Waterstaat, The Netherlands. Competition.
Zac Danton Office Tower, La Défense, Paris, France. Competition.
Leipziger Messe, Leipzig, Germany. Competition.

1992 Villa Dall'Ava, Saint Cloud, Paris, France.
Urban Design Forum, Yokohama, Japan. Project.
Kunsthal, Museum Park, Rotterdam, The Netherlands.
Educatorium, Utrecht, The Netherlands.
House in the Forest, The Netherlands.

1993 IJ-Oevers Master Plan, Amsterdam, The Netherlands.
Extension to the Stedelijk Museum, Amsterdam, The Netherlands. Competition.
Point City / South City, The Netherlands. Project

1994 2Bibliothèques de Jussieu, Paris, France. Competition.
Hypo Bank, Munich, Germany.
Maison â Bordeaux, France.
Cardiff Bay Opera House, Cardiff, UK. Competition.
Super and Popular, Groningen, The Netherlands.
Metro Dade Performing Arts Center, Miami, USA. Competition.
Saitama Arena, Tokio, Japan. Competition.
Tate Gallery Modern Art, London, UK. Competition.
Almere, Master Plan, Almere, The Netherlands.
Place des Nations, Genève, Switzerland. Competition.

1995 New Deal Residences, Amsterdam, The Netherlands.
C3 Towers, Rotterdam, The Netherlands.
Woningbouwfestival Housing, The Hague, The Netherlands.
A4 Highway Corridor. Rotterdam, The Netherlands. Project.
Seniorewoningen Housing, Alblasserdam, The Netherlands .
New Seoul International Airport, Seoul, Korea. Project.
T'Paard Cultural Center, The Hague, The Netherlands.
H-Project Masterplan, Seoul, Korea.

Zurich Airport, Zurich, Switzerland. Competition.
Stockholm Olympic Stadium, Stockholm, Sweden.
Togok Tower, Seoul, Korea. Project.
Luxor Theater, Rotterdam, The Netherlands.
Massena-Rive Gauche, Paris, France. Competition.
Villa Burnap, Palm Beach, USA.
Hotels and Apartments, The Hague, The Netherlands.
S, M, L, XL. Book.

1996 Chassé Campus, Breda, The Netherlands. Competition.
Breda Carré Buiding, Breda, The Netherlands.
Parking, Breda, The Netherlands.
Alliance Français, Rotterdam, The Netherlands.
SNU Museum, Seoul, Korea.
Pier Project, Thessaloniki, Greece. Project.
Maison des Droits de l'Homme, Genève, Switzerland. Competition.
Universal City Masterplan, Los Angeles, USA. Project.

1997 IIT, Chicago, USA. Competition.
Maasvlakte Master Plan, Rotterdam, The Netherlands.
Papendorp Master Plan, The Netherlands.
Hanoi New Master Plan, Hanoi, Vietnam.
Extension of the MOMA, New York, USA. Competition.
New Urbanism, Kassel, Germany. Exhibition.
Office Park, Düsseldorf, Germany. Project.
Zoetermeer Centrum West, The Netherlands, Project.
Lensvelt Showroom, Rotterdam, The Netherlands.
Netherlands Embassy, Berlin, Germany. Competition.
House, Berlin, Germany.

1998 Almere Block 6, Almere, The Netherlands.
El Baijo Bussiness & Cultural Center, Guadalajara, Mexico. Competition.
Santa Cruz de Tenerife Master Plan, Canary Islands, Spain. Competition.
Song-Do New Town, Inchon, Korea.
Second Stage Theater, New York, USA.
MAB-Tower, Rotterdam, The Netherlands.
Schiphol Airport Study, Amsterdam, The Netherlands. Project.
Living, Bordeaux, France. Exhibition.
MOCA, Roma, Italy, Competition.
Y2K House, Rotterdam, The Netherlands. Project

1999 Seatlle Public Library, Seatlle, USA.
Casa Da Musica, Porto, Portugal. Competition.
Philips Offices, Eindhoven, The Netherlands. Competition.
Zurich Satdium, Zurich, Switzerland. Competition.
Cities on the Move, London, UK. Exhibition.
30 Colours. Book.
Media Valley. Project.
Cita da Cultura, Santiago de Compostela, Spain. Competition.

2001 Cultural Center, Cordoba, Spain. Competition

2002 Prada Shop, New York, USA.
Guggenheim Museums, Las Vegas, USA.